33 HABITS
of a
Really
GOOD MAN

33 HABITS of a *Really* GOOD MAN

YVONNE SWINSON

Bonneville Books
Springville, Utah

ISBN 13: 978-1-59955-410-5

Published by Bonneville Books, an imprint of Cedar Fort Inc., 2373 W. 700 S., Springville, UT 84663
Distributed by Cedar Fort, Inc., www.cedarfort.com

LIBRARY OF CONGRESS CATALOGING-IN-PUBLICATION DATA

Swinson, Yvonne L. (Yvonne Leigh), 1970-
  33 habits of a really good man / Yvonne L. Swinson.
     p. cm.
   ISBN 978-1-59955-410-5
   1. Men—Conduct of life.I. Title. II. Title: Thirty-three habits of a
really good man.

 BJ1601.S95 2010
 170'.44—dc22

  2010008729

Cover design by Megan Whittier
Cover design © 2010 by Lyle Mortimer
Edited and typeset by Megan E. Welton

Printed in the United States of America

10 9 8 7 6 5 4 3 2 1

Printed on acid-free paper

To my mother:

"Behind every good man is

a good woman."

—Unknown

"We are **shaped and fashioned**

by those we love"

—Johann Wolfgang von Goethe

My father wrote the following in his journal:

"The people we love will shape our lives, if we let them. If someone really loves you they will help you become all that you are capable of becoming. They will not hold you back; they will always want what is best for you. Pick right, marry right, and you will never be sorry. **I PICKED RIGHT**."

I agree.

Contents

Acknowledgments

My thanks to Shara, who suggested changing our reading group to a reading/writing group, and to the other Washington Penholders for encouraging me to do this for more than just my children.

I thank the wonderful people at Cedar Fort, for helping this dream of mine come to fruition.

I acknowledge my sisters—the ones I have never known. Thank you for waiting patiently for your turn with Dad. Keep watch over him until we are all together again.

My deepest appreciation goes to my sisters who have let me tell this story as I remember it. Despite the absence of so many of their own memories, they have been full of encouragement and love.

A very special thanks to my grandparents, who raised for me a fine father, and to the many generations before them who passed along the good things.

I am full of gratitude for my amazing husband. My dad loved you as a son, and you loved him as a father. Thank you for never being intimidated by the size of his shadow.

Mostly I thank my children. You are the reason this was written. You will know too many years of your mortal life without your grandpa here to guide your steps as he did mine. May you always know how near he is, and when the distance seems too great, read on . . .

Introduction

My father kept a little black notebook full of quotes, proverbs, poems, and stories. They inspired him. They inspired us. We heard them so often they became a part of us. But he did more than just teach us words of wisdom. He took his own advice to heart, lived his life by it, and inspired others through his actions. And so, as a tribute to my father, I have taken a few of his favorite quotes and shared them here, along with the things he taught me.

I have done my best to find an original source for each quote. Unfortunately, many were paraphrased and many had evolved such that the original was impossible for me to find. My apologies and my thanks go to those who first spoke these wise words.

1. Speak Softly

My father taught me to speak softly. Well, he tried to teach me, I should say. It is the struggle of my life.

I honestly cannot remember a single time I heard my father yell. Raise his voice? Yes, once or twice. But yell? Never. Didn't happen.

I always assumed he was born with this uncanny ability to control his tongue. After his bleak diagnosis with lymphoma, he began putting together a personal history. Among the paperwork, we found a gift he had given my mother. It was a letter, written eight years into their marriage, which reads as follows:

Dear Barbara,

On this Christmas Day, I give to you the following:

1. The solemn vow that during the past eight years, I have been true and faithful. 2. That during the next year, I will give to you all my love and devotion. 3. That I

will try my best to be more patient and understanding of you and your needs. 4. That I will devote more time to helping you in rearing the children. 5. That I will try more diligently to control my temper and keep my voice down when correcting the children. 6. And finally, remember that all I have is yours and if you want it, all you need to do is ask.

"A soft answer **turneth away** wrath…"

Proverbs 15:1

I love you dearly, and will always do so, as long as you continue to treat me with the love and respect that you have over the past eight years.

Your loving husband, Bill

P.S. If at any time you feel that I am not living up to the above-mentioned things, you have the right to produce this, and I will immediately confess, say "I'm sorry," and correct the situation.

I don't know for sure, but I am guessing it was the nicest gift she ever received. As for me, once I got over the shock of reading the words "patience," "temper," and "keep my voice down," something wonderful dawned on me: there is hope for me yet.

Speaking of speech, my father did not care for swearing in any form. He didn't accept milder "substitute" words, nor did he care one bit for slang, which he felt was a sign of laziness. "Use your brain, Yvonne, and find the right word for what you want to say." We would come home from school with some "Holy Cow!" kind of expression, and in a flat, steady tone, he'd begin, "Swear not by the

"Swear not by **the heavens**, for that is where the Lord lives, swear not by **the earth**, for that is His footstool, but let your communication be solely Yea, yea or Nay, nay . . ."

Matthew 5:34–37
(as paraphrased by my father)

4

heavens . . ." and we would chime in, "for that is where the Lord lives . . ." Yeah, yeah.

Lest you think I exaggerate, let me take you back to an afternoon when I was a young teenager. Dad was in the garage working on a project when a hammer came down squarely on his thumb. Following the loud thud of the hammer hitting the floor, the only sound emanating from the garage was a loud, emphatic, "NAY, NAY, NAY, NAY, NAY!"

It didn't take long for co-workers and friends to learn of his distaste for such language. One day, a group of his co-workers had gathered in the boardroom for a staff meeting. Two latecomers came in laughing over a questionable joke, and the one encouraged the other to share the joke with the group. The second man refused, and the first man urged him on. The second man again refused, saying he couldn't tell the joke right then. The first man questioned him, "But why not? You just told me." The second man replied, "Because Bill Wells is in the room, that's why."

2.
Do Your
Best

My dad simply expected better of us than average, but it was more about effort than actual performance. He was the greatest fan to ever have at a sporting event because he knew from your face when your best was your best. And when you did your best, he cheered like there was no tomorrow. Never has a third-place medal received greater accolades than when the effort was apparent to my father.

Getting high marks in school was a priority in our home. I don't know if I was the first to bring home a grade that was considered substandard or not, but I do remember his response: "Is that your best?" That was his only question and my answer made all the difference. If I said, "No," I condemned myself. An honest "Yes" was all he required.

To my father, part of doing your best meant trying and trying and then trying again. "If at first you don't succeed . . ." he'd say with a smile. It meant persistence in following through. It meant "stick-to-it-iveness."

"Average is **just as close** to the bottom as it is to the top."

—Unknown

One of my favorite stories about Dad is one he told us years ago. He was working for a certain company as a salesman. While on a sales call, he went into a showroom to introduce himself. He said, "Hello, I'm Bill Wells, and I work for Such-and-such Company . . ." The showroom manager said, "Stop right there. The last experience I had with your company was lousy, and I don't want to talk to you. I don't want to hear from you. Leave." Dad picked up his briefcase and left. He walked outside. He set down his briefcase and straightened up his tie. And then he picked up his briefcase and went back in. The man said, "I thought I told you to leave." Dad said, "You did, but you didn't tell me I couldn't come back." He brought the man's business back to the company, and he and the man became good friends.

He was the type of man who stuck with tasks until they were finished, with problems until he conquered them, and with people until he won their confidence and love.

"Success is triumph—

a little 'try' and

a lot of 'umph.' "

—Unknown

3. Change begins with **me.**

My father was often a man of concise wisdom, even beyond the quotes and quips we were so familiar with. He didn't waste words. Less was more. I remember two particular incidents from my youth when so few words made such a large difference.

The first was when I was seventeen. Now, let me preface this by saying that there are a few people out there who will say I was a "difficult" teenager. If their reports are even partially true, then it is fair to add that my mother took the brunt of my "difficulty." I'm guessing in the disputes between us, she was right about 99 percent of the time.

But there was one day—one day I remember well—that

I *knew* I was right. I knew it, by golly, and I wasn't backing down for anything. My father came home in the middle of the stand-off. I was sitting at the kitchen table when he pulled up a chair. He waited for what seemed an eternity before he finally said, "Yvonne, I have been married to your mother for many years, and I have no power to change her. It doesn't matter how long you are her daughter, you will have no power to change her. Now, go change yourself." I have no idea what he did or did not say to my mother; I just remember my respect grew mightily for him that day because he didn't say that she was right. Of course, he didn't say that I was right, nor did he tell me how to fix the problem—he merely landed it squarely on my lap. I also cannot remember what I did to change. I'm guessing it involved a pretty serious attitude adjustment. One thing I do remember is that the thing that I really wanted and felt so right about that day eventually went my way.

The second incident happened a few years later. I went

off to Brigham Young University for four years, nearly finished my degree, and failed to find a husband, much to my parents' dismay. The truth was that my high school sweetheart had married another, and I wasn't over it yet. I was also up to my ears in debt and sick to death of the snow. I made the first of many stupid decisions. I came home, landed a good job and a lousy boyfriend, and never went back to school. Three years later, I was still wallowing in stupidity and wasn't very happy about it. My father, I guess, had seen enough. We sat in the backyard, staring at nothing for a long time before he finally said, "Yvonne, you're not happy. You will not find Mr. Right until you are Mrs. Right." And then he stood up and walked away.

Three months later, I met my husband.

"Watch the man behind the man in front of **you."**

—Unknown

4. I Can

I am drawn to stories about men like Dick Hoyt, the Super Dad who literally carries his disabled son mile after mile through the water and on the road in hundreds of marathons, triathlons, and other races—including six Ironman distance events. He decided he could. And he did.

But the man who first taught me an "I can" attitude was my father. In addition to hearing almost weekly, "If you think you can or you can't, you're right!" My father asked me on many occasions, "You can't? Or you won't?"

I had a gymnastics coach in my youth who was like-minded. The words "I can't" were forbidden in his gym, and the consequences were serious and immediate. "Two

> "If you think **you can** or **you can't**, you're right."
>
> —Henry Ford

hundred push ups!" he would bellow, and every time he said it, I would imagine my father smiling in the background.

To this day, the words "I can't" are not a part of my vocabulary. You may hear me say, "I struggle with . . ." or "I find it so hard to . . ." but it is a rare day indeed that I will dishonor my father with the words "I can't."

"Success comes **in cans**, failure comes in can'ts."

—Unknown

5. Stretch Your **Mind**

My father challenged us to think. Many a road trip was filled with hours of learning disguised as games. We sang songs, we played alphabet games in all their varieties, and we played "Password," "20 Questions," and "I Spy." Beyond all that, we memorized. We memorized Bible verses. We memorized songs. We memorized poetry. Not just simple Mother Goose rhymes, mind you, but long, narrative poetry. Go ahead, ask my sister to recite "The Faith of Little Mary": "The father, a well-digger, and strong was he as a father should be . . ." Or maybe you'd like to hear a spontaneous rendition of "The Touch of the Master's Hand": "T'was battered and scarred and the auctioneer thought it scarcely worth his while . . ." My favorite was "The Cremation of Sam McGee": "There are strange things done in the midnight sun by the men who moil for gold . . ."

To this day I count it a great blessing that I have the ability to memorize things easily. It is something I have challenged my own children to do, and I hope this skill serves them as well as it has served me. Go ahead, ask my daughter to recite the Twenty-third Psalm: "The Lord is my shepherd, I shall not want . . ."

"Vacant lots and vacant minds are **dumping grounds** for rubbish."

—Unknown

6. Be Punctual

To my father, it was a sign of disrespect to keep someone waiting. "Punctuality is just another form of courtesy," he would remind me. This was especially true with the Lord. How on Earth my father got three teenage girls and his wife out of the door and to church on time every Sunday for so many years, I cannot say. I just know he did it. This is something that runs so deep in my bones that I have become convinced there is an "always on time for church" gene, and I got it from Dad. For as long as I can remember, I have never been late to church. Not once, ever. The few times I wasn't ten minutes early are true exceptions. On those Sundays, I sometimes think I hear my father "tick-tick-ticking" in my ear. From the moment the clock hits "ten minutes 'til," my heart races, my palms sweat, and my blood pressure rises. It's weird, I know, but it's true.

Dad was equally firm about curfews. We were allowed to negotiate our curfew right up until the moment we left the house, but once the time

> "If you're not **ten minutes early** you're late."
>
> —A variation of an old military adage

was set, we simply were not late. We knew better than to keep him waiting. The consequence? One week's grounding for every minute past curfew. I only faced the music once. (It wasn't my fault, I promise.) I had tried to sneak in the back window, but Dad was waiting. For some unknown reason, mercy prevailed, but I knew I'd used my last "get out of jail free" card. I was never out past curfew again.

7.
Ingenuity

My father was recognized for thinking outside the box. Many a time when a solution seemed nowhere to be found, Dad would come up with something inventive, new, and clever. One of the best illustrations of my dad's ingenuity was the way he handled a good, old-fashioned yard sale. He would often take paper lunch sacks and grab two or three small items he knew would never sell alone, place them in a bag, and staple it shut. He would then make a sign—"Surprise Grab Bags: $.25"—and sell them all morning.

At another yard sale, my father had a large pile of scrap lumber that he didn't really want to haul to the dump. He took a dozen or so good two-by-fours and placed them on top of the pile with a sign that said, "Lumber for Sale." A gentleman approached and asked the price of the two-by-fours. My father said with a grin "I'll give you that whole pile of lumber for $5.00." The man corrected him quickly, "Oh, no. I only want the two-by-fours." Dad replied, "Well, then, that'll cost you ten," whereupon the man hauled away the whole pile of scrap.

"Don't be so narrow minded that your **ears cause friction.**"

—Unknown

8. Seek Truth

We grew up Mormon in the Bible Belt. At times, this was a really bad combination. We heard a lot of anti-Mormon rhetoric and often it led to questions, but this never seemed to trouble my father. He either already had, or was willing to find, an answer to all of our questions. But usually he would preface his answers by saying, "If you want to sell me a Ford, don't tell me what's wrong with a Chevy."

"You never **find truth** in studying error."

—Unknown

9. Love Is Action

My father was a giver. He was a server, which was usually apparent in the little things, like opening a door for someone or giving a bright smile to a stranger. Other times, it was bigger—like his ever-willing, ever-faithful service in the Church. Those closest to him saw it most often. Love was action, pure and simple.

The most touching example of this was in his last days as he lay in a hospital bed approaching death. He quietly slipped the nurse some money and asked her to pick out some birthday flowers for my mother.

"Do **all the good** you can, in all the ways you can, in **all the places** you can, and **all the times** you can, to **all the people** you can, for as long as you ever can."

—John Wesley

10. Don't Take Offense

Dad always said that life was too short to take offense. He believed that taking offense hurt you more than the other guy anyway. He simply did not waste time being angry. He lived by Abraham Lincoln's philosophy—he destroyed his enemies by making them into friends.

I will add that one of the most healing moments of my life was when I finally let go of the anger I had against a man who had done me serious wrong. I had carried the grief and hurt and anger and hatred—offense, if you will—for many years, when a very wise man suggested simply "Hasn't he hurt you enough already? Every day you are angry or hurt or sad is one more day you've given him." These were words my father would have truly appreciated. I honored Dad by taking the advice. A great weight was lifted, and I haven't been the same since.

"He who takes offense when **none is intended** is a fool. He who takes offense when it is intended is **also a fool.**"

—Paraphrasing Brigham Young, who was possibly quoting an earlier source

11.
Choose to
Be Happy

Dad chose to be happy all the time.

In response to the typical question "How are you?" his response was never just a simple, "Fine."

He was always a bright, energetic "Great!" or "Wonderful!" or "Happy!"

He often roused us for the day with his bright (if slightly off-tune) version of "Oh, what a beautiful morning, oh what a beautiful *daayyy*!"

He used to say "If you don't feel like smiling, just try it for a while, and you'll soon feel like it."

He liked happy faces. There is a pillowcase he used that is still hanging around somewhere. It is covered in bright, neon, smiley faces. He loved it, and now my son has adopted it whenever a sleepover at Grandma's is in order.

Nurses hung out in Dad's room a little longer than necessary, because he was such a happy patient, even when he was feeling his worst.

What a glorious thing it is to be happy. And what a wonderful gift indeed that it is something we can choose to be.

"Happiness is **an inside job**. We do not find joy and happiness, we make them."

—Unknown

12.
Nurture

One of the most vivid memories of my youth is one in which my father was a nurturer when I was sick with croup. In my mind's eye, I was only four or five, but in reality, I had to have been at least eight, because that was when we moved to Atlanta. The house we lived in had a large, wrap-around deck on the upper floor. In those days, the remedy for a child with croup was the cool, moist, evening air. My father would wrap me in a slightly scratchy purplish-bluish-greenish afghan that my grandmother had made. Then he would carry me out onto the deck and begin his steady, rocking gait from one end of the deck to the other and back again and again and again.

This is one of those few, precious memories that impressed itself upon my every sense. I can still see the tiny glint of night stars and hear the sound of my father's shoes tap-tapping on the wood of the deck. I can still feel the woolly yarn against my skin and smell and taste the sweet humidity in the air. But there was something more— something I can barely explain, except to say that in those moments I sensed love, deep and sure.

I saw, heard, smelled, touched, and tasted love in the arms of my father as he held me quietly in the night.

"The sound of **a kiss** is not so loud as that of **a cannon**, but its echo will last a great deal longer."

—Oliver Wendell Holmes

13. Dream BIG

My father always set goals, and he encouraged us to do the same. But he didn't particularly care for easy-to-reach ambitions. Another little adage we heard a lot of was "Reach for the stars, and you will not come up with a handful of dirt."

So what if what we wanted to do was impossible? Striving for the impossible would usually bring great results. Partly because he was a big dreamer, he was a huge success in his work. He would set an enormous goal, go about doing it, and even if he came up short, it was often better than anything expected or even imagined.

I believe one of the problems in the world today is the lack of big dreamers. Yes, they are out there—but for every man who walks on the moon, breaks the four-minute mile, or composes a masterpiece, there are hundreds or even thousands of others who are satisfied with mediocrity. One of the prayers of my heart is to never settle for such but to hitch my wagon to that star and somehow, someday find a way.

"Bite off more than you can chew, and chew it. Plan to do more than you can do, and do it! Hitch your **wagon to a star**, keep your seat, and there you are."

—A Joint Effort between Anonymous and Ralph Waldo Emerson

14. Laugh **Often**

With this topic, I run the risk of turning this little memoir into hundreds of pages. My dad's greatest gift, I believe, was his sense of humor. He was a Bill Cosby sort of dad. He loved practical jokes, funny stories, and being a goofball. You couldn't be around him very long without enjoying a good chuckle. It would be sad to miss even one funny story, but here are just a few that still make me smile.

As children, he tucked us in at night with a strange tradition we referred to simply as The Kitty. The Kitty would come scratching on the door, meow, and screech his way across the room and then leap onto the bed in a fit of purring and tickling until we laughed ourselves half to death. I remember one night when I was about fifteen. The Kitty had not visited in many years, but I was way too cool for that stuff anyway. Sure enough, that night I heard a scratch-scratching at the door. I was mortified. I determinedly pretended to be asleep. The Kitty was persistent. And loud. And he screeched and meowed right in my ear over and over as I pinched my lips and eyes together as tightly as possible. And then he stopped. After a long silence, I thought I'd won. Then I felt Dad's breath right in my ear as he whispered an urgent "Oink!" We laughed until our sides ached, and then we laughed some more.

Later on, while in high school, I had a huge crush on a fellow in my science class. I spent nearly a year in this smitten condition before we finally got together for a study "date." I introduced him to my father. "Dad, this Steve. Steve, this is my dad." Dad looked from Steve to me and back again. Then he looked my way and said simply, "Yvonne, he's not ugly."

All of our dates were treated to his unique sense of humor. Sometimes he greeted them in interesting costumes. He would black a tooth. He would wear a sneaker on one foot and a dress shoe on the other. He would come in the room all hunched over and dragging one foot behind him muttering "Hiya, Bob! "Howyadoin, Bob?" with a funny lisp. He would douse them with water machine guns, overfill their glasses at the table, and make bets with them that usually resulted in water-soaked britches. They never got enough. And neither did we.

"Do not take life seriously; you'll never get out alive."

—Van Wilder

15. Have Fun

Dad never cared if people thought he was goofy. He'd take the little shopping basket at the grocery store, drape it over his arm, and skip down the aisles singing loudly, "A tisket, a tasket . . ." "Daa-aaddd!!!" we would hiss in his general direction. "Oh, who cares," he'd reply. "You'll never see any of these people again anyway"

He installed a speaker behind the grill of the old station wagon and wired it to the CB radio. As we drove down the streets of our neighborhood, whenever some ornery teenager on a skateboard refused to yield the right-of-way my father picked up the handset and bellowed through the speaker, "GET OUT OF THE WAY!" And boy, did that teenager suddenly move. We ducked down to avoid being seen. "Don't worry about it. You'll never see him again anyway . . ."

We went to a fast food restaurant one day. The food was good and the staff was nice, so my dad asked to speak to the manager. He raved about the good food, service, and so forth and then pulled a good friend's business card out of his pocket. The friend worked for a corporation that was the parent company to this particular fast food chain. Then my father said "My name is Steve Jones, and I work for X Company. If you will call my office collect on Monday morning, I will send you a free computer." How he did it with a straight face is beyond me. Mom scolded and Dad responded, "We'll never see him again anyway." The funniest part of this particular story came around years later, when we travelled back through that old town and had dinner with Steve Jones and his family. The conversation turned to prank phone calls, and Steve slapped the table and said he had the one to beat all. "Someone called my office one morning—collect!—and told me I owed him a computer . . ."

My father never faced the front of an elevator. He just

stepped inside and instead of turning around, he pressed the button for where he was headed and then stood there, facing everyone else. If we were with him, we were never sure what to do, but you may have guessed his response: "Just smile, Yvonne . . ."

"You'll never **see them again** anyway."

—Bill Wells

16. Know When to **Stop Talking**

Enough said.

"To avoid trouble and ensure safety, **breathe through your nose**; it keeps your mouth shut."

—Unknown

"When you get **in deep water**, keep your mouth shut."

—Unknown

17.
Do Your
Part

My father didn't pass the buck. He dug in with all his might and did everything he could.

This revealed itself most often in a church setting. We were taught not to turn down opportunities for service, and he encouraged us to volunteer. If everyone did that, where would the Church be? He paid generous offerings. If everyone did that, where would the Church be? Oh, and remember the punctuality thing? Yup, if everyone was on time, where would this Church be?

But it didn't just apply to church—whether at work, home, or play, the philosophy applied. We heard variations of this all the time—what if everyone left their shopping carts wherever they pleased? What if everyone decided to cut out ten minutes early? What if everyone picked just one flower?

I'm embarrassed at times to answer these questions:

If every member of this family were just like me . . . ? If every neighbor was just like me . . . ? If every friend was just like me . . . ? If everyone in the world was just like me . . . ?

Maybe I can't change the world. But I am obligated to do well with my little corner of it.

"If every member of the Church was **just like me**, what kind of a church would this Church be?"

—Unknown

18. Work to **Learn**

Dad was not an educated man—not by the world's standards, anyway. But he was a man of much learning. We had a wonderful library in our home, and he was always reading something. He was also comfortable highlighting and writing in his books. I just love finding a book he has scribbled his thoughts in and putting myself in his shoes as I read.

As we grew older and came to him with our many questions, he never dismissed us or shrugged his shoulders. He was generally as interested in the answer as we were. It was this kind of training that led me to the owner's manual rather than the telephone the first time I blew out a tire.

He encouraged us to be college-educated, and he showed an interest in the subjects we were studying. I remember more than once, when I was finished with a semester at school, sending my textbooks home for him to read. We had delightful conversations that expanded what my professors taught me.

"God has created us with **two ends**: one to think with and one to sit on. Heads you win, **tails you lose**."

—Unknown

When I was asked to be a Sunday school teacher for my local congregation, he studied the material right along with me and called me with neat quotes or tidbits on the lesson topics.

In his last years, his reading and study became more fervent. It was a common thing to see him at his desk with his nose in a book. His body did not feel well, but his mind still wanted to be stretched.

19. Learn to **Work**

My father worked hard for his living and we knew it. He was not the kind of man that took another man's work for granted either. In other words, he did not leave his dirty clothes on the floor for Mom to pick up.

And he taught us to work. Mother, of course, dealt out the inside chores, but Dad taught me to cut the grass and change the oil. He wanted us to be able to do things for ourselves, should the need arise. It was this kind of training that led me to the owner's manual instead of the telephone the first time I blew out a tire. Oh, wait, I already said that, didn't I?

My father was a generous man, but not in the sense that he handed us things on

> "Nothing works **unless** you do."
>
> —Nido Qubein

a silver platter. He could have bought me a car when I turned sixteen, but instead he took me to the car lot, he gave his advice, and he stood proudly by as I handled my first adult transaction. I still have a copy of the check I wrote as a down payment on that first car proudly displayed in an old scrapbook.

> "What we **obtain too cheap**, we esteem too lightly."
>
> —Thomas Paine

> "Big men are only **average men motivated** to action."
>
> —Vernon Law

I also remember when I went off to school and started spending foolishly, getting myself into the hot water of heavy debt fast. He was willing to help—in the form of a loan—*if* I was willing to give him a budget in writing.

20. Think More about the **Other Fellow**

My father was a prime example of this principle in his marriage, but it was also evident in his work.

I remember once, after he unexpectedly lost his job, one of my sisters suggested he might consider marketing the latest, greatest line of cosmetics. People were making big money in that field, and he was a good salesman. He wouldn't consider it. He didn't believe in $50 mascara. He simply would not sell a product he didn't believe in. If it wasn't good for the other fellow, he didn't want to make money off of it.

He developed a reputation for looking out for his customers. Often this resulted in a level of trust that was almost unbelievable. One of his customers once said that if it were possible, he'd just let Dad take over his life and make every decision for him, for he knew he'd come out better than making the decisions himself.

"Marriage is not 50/50— it's 100/100. You both try to give 100 percent every day, and if one or both of you fall a little short, you **still come out ahead.**"

—Bill Wells

21. Don't Worry

Why waste time worrying? This went hand in hand with his continual optimism. I suppose he worried sometimes, but it was never evident to us. My father's approach was very practical: envision the worst scenario, decide how you would handle it, and then move on. Plan for the worst, expect the best. Simple, right?

Sometimes this approach became downright funny. Once, when I was about to go on a first date, I was worried. "What about?" he asked. "I dunno. What if I do something stupid?" I said. "Like what?" he replied. "Like throw up all over him or something," I exclaimed, exasperated. "Well, what if you did?" he said with a grin. "I would *die!*" "Well, then you'd be dead. Worse things to be. Besides, that should be my worry, not yours . . ."

"What if my husband loses his job?" "Well, what if he

does?" "What if something's wrong with the baby" "Well, what if there is?"

Don't misunderstand, this wasn't flippant or callous in any way—just extremely practical-minded. If we can make a plan for the worst-case scenario, there is always a cathartic mental response: the absence, or near-absence, of worry.

"Worrying is like **a rocking chair.** It gives you something to do but it doesn't get you anywhere."

—Van Wilder

22.
Optimism

Along with preparing for the worst came expecting the best. My father always did. I have known of few people in my life who could match my father's optimism. He simply refused to take a gloomy view. I can't even begin to tell you how many times I heard "Well, on the bright side . . ."

This never-failing optimism, I'm afraid, may have contributed to his lack of preparation for the inevitable when he became seriously ill. I know for sure that it contributed to mine. You see, we never realized just how bad he was feeling, because he refused to wear it on his face. And so, riding on Dad's optimism, we assumed things were better than they were. Only after his passing, as we read through his journal, did it become apparent to us just how bad he'd been feeling for a startling amount of time.

When I sat by my mother in the hospital that dark day

when the doctor solemnly said, "Barbara, he's not going to be going home this time," I was dumbfounded. After the initial shock wore off, he quietly smiled at me and asked me to please take mother to pick out a grave site.

Even then, as my husband sat at his bedside and asked "Are you scared?" he answered without hesitation, "No. I do not want to die, but I am not afraid of dying." I imagine that is because the heaven he saw coming was like the silver lining he saw all along.

"Every cloud has a silver lining, if **we provide the sunshine.**"

—Unknown

23.
Priorities

My father traveled a great deal when we were kids. He was on the road a lot. He went out of town first thing Monday morning and rarely got back before Friday night. But we knew as soon as he walked through the door, he was ours. Nothing that wasn't absolutely necessary would interfere with our weekends together. He made that time ours, and it was quality time.

The last day that my father was lucid, my husband had the great privilege of spending a couple of hours alone in conversation with him. One of the questions he asked was "What is your biggest regret?" "I wish I'd spent more time with the girls." Dad answered. Steve went on to ask, "Bill, your daughters love and honor you deeply. How did you do that?" "I spent time with them," was his simple reply.

"You will never **find
time for anything.**
If you want time, you
must make it."

—Charles Buxton

24.
Speak Well
of **Others**

I am sure there were people that my dad wasn't crazy about, but he always spoke well of and kindly to everyone. He did not like gossip. He didn't pass it on.

There were times I felt a complaint against someone was well deserved. Instead, I was often surprised to find my dad defending the person or finding something positive to say.

If I came home grumbling about someone, my father was quick to point out that I didn't know the whole story. His

"Two things are **bad for the heart**— running up stairs and running down people."

—Bernard M. Baruch

standard reply was always, "Give them the benefit of the doubt."

> ## "The best way to make **a mountain** out of a molehill is to add a little dirt."
>
> —Unknown

On extremely rare occasions, I would hear him voice a brief objection about someone. But his tone was almost always one of disappointment rather than contempt: "Oh, I wish he wouldn't do that."

He reminded me to look for the good in people and to speak it out loud as often as possible. He told me once, and it really stuck with me, "If you want to give a true compliment to a person, tell someone else who you know will repeat it to them. Sometimes a compliment said directly to a person is perceived as merely being polite. But if you like something enough to tell a third party, they'll always know it's sincere." He added, "Oh, and if you ever hear a compliment about someone else, be sure to pass it on."

25. Know Where You're **Going**

So often, at moments of decision, my father would ask simply, "Where are you going, Yvonne? Will that decision get you there?"

Or, "Is that what you want most, Yvonne, or what you want now?"

One of my all-time favorite books is *Little Britches*, by Ralph Moody. My father would have loved it too, had he ever read it. The author, like me, had a pretty amazing father. The book recounts some of the many lessons his father taught him, including the following:

> While mother and the others were getting supper fixed, Father and I sailed the boat down the creek. At a place where the current wasn't too swift, and where there was pretty good breeze, Father said, "You know, a man's life

"When a **man** doesn't know what **harbor** he is making, no **wind** is right."

—Unknown

is a lot like a boat. If he keeps his sail set right it doesn't make too much difference which way the wind blows or which way the current flows. If he knows where he wants to go and keeps his sail trimmed carefully he'll come into the right port. But if he forgets to watch his sail till the current catches him broadside he's pretty apt to smash up on the rocks."

Dad would have nodded his agreement.

26. Be Clean

My father was a tidy man. His car was tidy, his desk was tidy, his shirt was generally tucked in. But more than believing in physical tidiness, he believed in spiritual tidiness. A clean life felt good, pure and simple.

A good friend came to visit him in the hospital. By the time he arrived, the illness and the medications had taken enough effect that Dad was no longer communicating. His eyes were closed. We were not sure how much, if anything, he was aware of.

The friend and I sat talking of children and their adventures and the messes they make. We laughed for a moment or two as he spoke of his young mess-maker, and the

> "Cleanliness **is next to** Godliness."
> —Ancient Proverb

> "We act **the way we dress**—untidy dress shows an untidy mind."
>
> —Unknown

spilled milk and scattered toys he'd been dealing with.

The friend finally stood to leave, bid his farewells to my non-responsive father, and walked out of the room. Just as he passed through the doorway, Dad blurted out, "Clean up after yourself, and you'll always have friends." The surprised friend turned around to see Dad still lying there, eyes closed in apparent slumber. We chuckled. The message came through loud and clear. And we both knew he was talking about a lot more than spilled milk and toys.

27. Sing

I have no musical ability. Really, I don't. None at all. I was actually kicked out of the sixth grade band. Nevertheless, my father taught me to sing. "Yvonne," he said, "the scripture says, 'make a *joyful* noise,' not 'make a beautiful noise.'"

I remember going to church as a kid and eagerly opening up the hymn book to see what we'd be singing. I always hoped for a song with a two-part chorus. "God be With You Till We Meet Again" was my favorite. I'd sing high, "Till we Mee-ee-eeet . . ." and he'd sing low, "Till we meet." To this day I cannot sing that song without straining my ears to hear one of the men in the congregation take the low part.

I honestly have no idea whether my father had any vocal talent at all. If he did, I was certainly the worst possible judge of it. If he didn't? Well, to me he sounded like an angel.

"Make a joyful noise . . ."

The book of Psalms,
seven times

28. Be Humble

Humility is a hard thing to describe.

Those who think they are humble rarely are. My father was humble, without a doubt. Me? Um, not so much. Especially in my younger years.

Dad often reminded me, "No one is ever so good that they need no advice," or "There's always room for improvement," or "Don't be afraid of criticism, Yvonne, you can always learn something from it," or simply, "Don't get too big for your britches."

My father sought opportunities for growth—not just because he was a goal setter or a big dreamer, but because he really did wish to be taught. Something of that attitude shone in his eyes—a very visible kind of humility, if you will.

The paradox of being humble and teachable is that people who attain such are always looked to by others as teachers—and so it was with Dad.

"Be careful about calling yourself an expert. An 'ex' is a has-been and a 'spurt' is a drip under pressure."

—Unknown

29. Lose the Stubborn **Streak**

If there is one thing I got from the Oliver side of the family, it's the stubborn streak. On occasion, it served me well. I was persistent when it came to learning a new skill in gymnastics. I was downright determined to win come spelling bee time, and I usually succeeded. I was absolutely fixed in my standards, and thus avoided much of the high school drinking scene.

But then there were other times— oh, must I confess?

"Some people are like **cement:** all mixed up and permanently set."

—Unknown

68

Apparently, it started when I was just a tiny thing, obstinately refusing to pick up my shoes.

Well, let's just say that Dad saw the fault better than anyone, and much of his counsel to me revolved around it. Usually it required a total shift in thinking. He insisted that I at least *try* to see things from another view, walk a mile in another's shoes, so to speak. And of course, when I did, my mindset would change.

Ironic, isn't it, that the thing which most frustrates me in others is the very thing I display the most? It is hard, indeed, to admit when "don't give up" has been replaced with "don't give in."

> "Some people are like **tacks**. We will go no further than our heads will let us."
>
> —Unknown

30. Slow Down a **Little**

One little quote on the pages of Dad's little scribble spoke to me in a particularly powerful way: "The greatest suffering in the world is regret."

It is fair to say that my father taught me well as far as work was concerned. I have often read the story of Mary and Martha in the New Testament. There is a part of me that gets frustrated with the story, for I am a Martha. I want to say, "Well, Mary, just help her out for a few minutes and when the work is done, you can both sit at the Savior's feet." The other part of me knows all too well that the work is never done.

As far as slowing down a little, my father developed a far better balance than I have. He knew how to stop and smell the roses. He enjoyed the quiet, still moments of life. He could sit and do nothing and soak it up and savor it.

Not long after he died, I had a dream. He sat in an armchair beside a small table and beckoned me to sit in the chair beside him. I barely slowed at the doorway.

"Can I get you something, Dad?"

"No, honey, just come and flip a penny with me."

"Sure, Dad, but are you sure you don't want anything first?"

"No, no, I'm fine. Just sit and flip a penny with me."

"Can I just get you a glass of milk?"

Abruptly the dream ended, and he was gone. I woke to bitter tears. I knew in my soul that the dream would have lingered had I only paused from my Martha-like attitude. I was invited three times, and three times I'd failed to respond. Oh, to have flipped a penny for just a moment or two . . .

"The **greatest suffering** in the world **is regret.**"

—Unknown

31. Pray Often

My father's first encounter with cancer was when I was fifteen. The lump near his armpit was bound to be benign, or so the doctors said. When they came back saying breast cancer, we were taken aback to say the least.

The days that followed were filled with fasting and prayer. The following Sunday in church, my father shared with the congregation his testimony about the power of prayer. He related how helpless he felt when he first heard the diagnosis. But he went on to say that as he came to each of our rooms that evening to tuck us in, he happened to find each one of us kneeling in prayer. He bore

"Prayer should be **the key of the day** and the lock of the night."

—George Herbert

witness of the power of a child's prayer and how our faith sustained him at a moment when he felt weak.

I penned a little poem shortly thereafter and share it with you now:

My child, tonight I saw you
There kneeling in the night,
Gleaming in your tear-filled eyes
A bit of heaven's light.
I saw that 'round your golden head
An angel's halo shone,
And clasped between your tiny fists
A faith far past my own.
"Become as little children"
I've heard the Savior say
I finally understood him
As I stood and watched you pray.
I turned and went into my room
And fell upon my knees
And asked for God to help me find
The little child in me.

Twenty years later, I sat beside him in the ICU, thinking death was approaching. We had another year, but I didn't know it then. As I sat there, the words of my poem changed quite suddenly:

> Father, tonight I saw you
> Your eyes a sparkling light
> The kind of light from deep within
> That shines through blackest night.
> I saw that 'round your blessed head
> An angel's halo shines
> And clasped between your aging hands
> A faith surpassing mine.
> And yet I know, however weak
> My faith in God is true
> For every lesson learned from Him
> I've learned by following you.
> Indeed, you found me on my knees
> Those many years ago
> And often since I've knelt again,
> Because you taught me so.

"Don't ask the Lord to guide your steps unless you're **willing to move** them."

—Christian Proverb

32.
Make It
a **Habit**

As I near the end of this little account, I can't help but say what my dad would have said: "It does no good to learn a thing if you don't retain it—no better way to learn a behavior than to make it a habit." As I review the preceding pages, I lament the fact that many of the good things he taught me are not yet habits in my life.

But after all, there is hope for me yet.

"Good **habits** are to success what **rails** are to a train."

—Unknown

"Bad habits are like **a comfortable bed:** easy to get into and hard to get out of."

—Unknown

33. Love

He said it often.
And he meant it.
I love you too, Dad.

"I love you."

Yvonne Swinson and her father, Bill Wells

Yvonne Leigh (Wells) Swinson was born in North Carolina and spent her childhood moving around the Southeastern states. An enthusiastic reader at an early age, she has read thousands of books and one of her (many) childhood dreams was to write her own. She now lives in Washington, Utah, with her husband and five children. Her other passions include coaching gymnastics, hiking the great outdoors, and homeschooling.

The Wagon Train West

McGraw Hill SRA

Columbus, OH

SRAonline.com

 SRA

Send all inquiries to this address:
SRA/McGraw-Hill
4400 Easton Commons
Columbus, OH 43219

ISBN: 978-0-07-608780-8
MHID: 0-07-608780-8

1 2 3 4 5 6 7 8 9 NOR 13 12 11 10 09 08 07

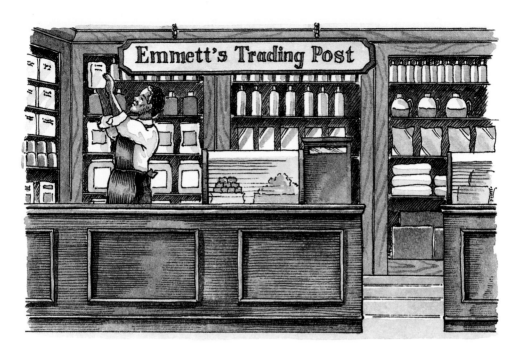

The year was 1845, and people were flocking to the West like flies to a pie at a picnic. All kinds of people—white, black, big, skinny, tall, short—were going. One thing they all had in common was Emmett's Trading Post in St. Louis. They either stopped there or started there—it didn't matter which—but they all needed provisions, and that's what Emmett had to offer.

Business at Emmett's had picked up quite a bit lately. Emmett himself had considered taking off for the West, where he had heard that the sky was bluer than the bluest blue and bigger than anything he had ever seen in his lifetime. He did not know, though, because his papa had told him over and over again to finish what he had started. And since he had started this business, he wanted to see it through.

One afternoon while Emmett was waiting on a customer, he started thinking things over, though. There was a wagon train departing in the morning—one of the last ones that would come by for a little while. He had come to St. Louis in the hopes of finding something bigger and better for himself, and he had, but he had a hankerin' for more. He knew his papa would have understood this and knew he would have been proud of Emmett's adventurous spirit. Emmett made the decision to join the wagon train.

He gave the keys to the store to his friend Jeremiah. The wagon master told him the train was pulling out at dawn. The man said, "As long as yer ready to go, you can come along, but don't be 'specting us to wait for you."

Emmett assured the wagon master that he would be ready in two shakes of a lamb's tail. The wagon master shook his head, thinking that Emmett could not possibly be ready on time.

The wagon master didn't know Emmett, though.

That night when the store closed, Emmett got to work. He hitched his oxen to his wagon and began loading it up. Like a whirlwind at work, Emmett threw supplies into the wagon faster than the winds of a twister. (That's a tornado to you cityfolk.)

When dawn came Emmett had eight hundred pounds of flour, seven hundred pounds of bacon, two hundred pounds of beans, one hundred pounds of fruit, seventy-five pounds of coffee, and twenty-five pounds of salt in his wagon. He hoped it would be enough to feed him for at least the first week of the trip. Emmett was a big man with an even bigger appetite.

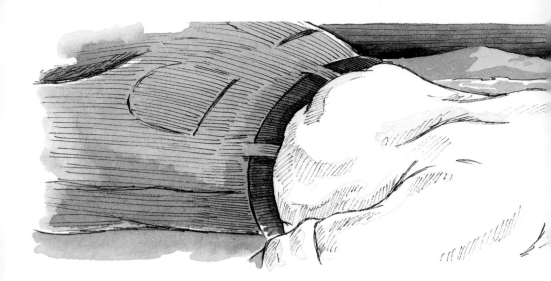

The wagon train set off across the Midwest prairie with the two dozen wagons embarking together. For the first few weeks, things moved along just fine—slow, but fine. The wagon scout left every morning and reported back to the wagon master about what was up ahead for the next day's journey. Life was sweeter than Mama's gooseberry jam.

Then the weather started changing a bit, and it rained much more than usual. That contributed to the change in pace, making it even slower. Since most everybody walked alongside their wagons, the mud made for a big mess and slowed them up even more.

One night the scout came back and said, "That there Kansas River is flooded up ahead. I'm a-feared we'll all drown!"

The wagon master thought and thought and, shaking his head, said he would sleep on it and figure it out in the morning.

Emmett overheard the wagon scout's report. He knew what he had to do, and he set about doing it. While everyone was asleep, he tiptoed out of the camp and trotted off toward the river. It was flooded, all right, but did that stop Emmett? No how, no way! He simply lay down on the ground and opened his mouth. The water from the flooded river flowed in, and Emmett swallowed and swallowed and swallowed. The river receded, and the water went down, down, down. By the time he stood up, you could not tell there had been a flood. He had even spat out the fishes that had been swirling in the rushing waters.

The next morning when the wagon train arrived at the river, they were able to make the crossing without a hitch.

Days passed and the air near the mountains grew chilly. Emmett had heard rumors that the weather on this trail could get really bad, and he shivered just thinking about it. Folks said the snowflakes on the trail were as big as quilts but not nearly as warm. Emmett supposed that that was where the expression "blanketed by snow" came from. So he was not surprised when the scout came back to the wagon train one night, talking about a terrible snowstorm ahead. He said the snow was coming down faster than a swarm of bees after honey and that he had gotten caught in it. The icicle on the end of his nose quivered as he said, "I'm a-feared we'll lose the trail!"

The wagon master thought and thought and, shaking his head, said he would sleep on it and figure it out in the morning.

Again Emmett heard the scout and the wagon master talking. Emmett knew what he had to do, and he set about doing it. While everyone was asleep, he tiptoed out of the camp and trotted off around the bend. It had snowed, all right—musta been a ragin' blizzard from what he could tell—but did that stop Emmett? No how, no way! He rubbed his arms and then his hands to warm up. He stomped his feet to get the circulation back to flowin' in his frozen toes, took a couple of deep breaths, and exhaled. He blew and he blew and he blew—matter of fact, he blew all the snow clear off the trail and then some.

The next morning when the procession got around the bend, instead of snow there was a pristine trail awaiting them. The wagon master began to think his scout might be having trouble with his eyesight.

Time passed uneventfully. The land was rough and bumpy, and the wagon train had to move slowly. Everyone was tired and hungry—their feet ached from all the walking they had to do, and they were sick of bacon and beans.

Then one evening the wagon scout returned to camp with some devastating news. The trail they were on would take them through a pass in the Rocky Mountains. But the pass was obstructed with fallen rock, dirt, and debris, built up to a point that the scout feared they would not get through. He said, "I figure that snowstorm set off an avalanche or somethin'. I'm a-feared we'll never make it!"

The wagon master thought and thought and, shaking his head, said he would sleep on it and figure it out in the morning.

As Emmett was settling in for a night's sleep, he overheard the wagon master and the scout discussing the mountain pass. He was mighty exhausted, but Emmett knew what he had to do, and he set about doing it. While everyone was asleep, he tiptoed out of the camp and trotted off toward the Rocky Mountains. The debris blocking the path was high, all right, but did that stop Emmett? No how, no way! He spit in his calloused hands and rubbed them together. Then he grabbed the shovel he had brought and began to dig. He dug and he dug and he dug, and soon the mountain pass was excavated and cleared of all the fallen debris.

The next morning the wagon train headed for the mountain pass and found it level, clean, and altogether crossable. The wagon master shook his head at the scout.

More time passed. The expedition was more than halfway to its destination. The womenfolk talked about strawberries in California bigger than a large man's fist, and the menfolk discussed steaks that extended across the whole top of a fancy restaurant table. Children spoke of ocean waves so high you needed a ladder to climb back down.

The scout left for his ride and came back that night with terrible news. All the melting snow and rain had washed out a bridge that the wagon train had to cross to get over a huge river. He said, "I done rode up and down the bank for miles and miles. There ain't no way to cross. I'm a-feared we'll drown … again!"

The wagon master thought and thought and, shaking his head, said he would sleep on it and figure it out in the morning.

Once again Emmett overheard the conversation. He knew what he had to do, and he set about doing it. While everyone was asleep, he tiptoed out of the camp and trotted off toward the river, looking for the washed-out bridge. He found pieces of it scattered here and there, as if a giant hand had picked them up and tossed them in the air—but did that stop Emmett? No how, no way! He took a few deep breaths and pulled and pulled and pulled down trees from the nearby forest. He dove into the pile and worked so fast you would have missed it if you blinked. Before you knew it, Emmett had woven a sturdy bridge that extended from one bank of the river to the other.

The next morning the wagon train was able to make it over the river. The wagon master mumbled under his breath, "That scout …"

The bad weather seemed to be behind them. The days were getting longer, the sun was getting warmer, and the wagon train was almost there. Good thing too, because everyone was almost out of fresh drinking water.

The scout panicked one night, yelling, "How are we gonna make it through the desert with no water?"

The wagon master held a meeting and told everyone on the wagon train that the water they had left had to be rationed.

People began offering up ideas about just how to do that. Water for this, no water for that, only a little water here and there for this and that, and so on. There were too many suggestions, and only some of them made a lick of sense at all.

The wagon master thought and thought and, shaking his head, said he would sleep on it and figure it out in the morning.

The meeting disbanded, and everyone headed back to their wagons for the night. Emmett knew what he had to do, and he set about doing it. While everyone was asleep, he grabbed up a few ladles and empty water barrels and tiptoed out of the camp. He knew that the closest place for water was a lake that was a long way off, but did that stop Emmett? No how, no way! He took off, running as fast as he could, leaving a cloud of dust behind him. When he got to the lake, he scooped and scooped and scooped up water until every single barrel was full, and then he headed back to camp.

When the pioneers woke up in the morning, a barrel full of water was sitting next to each wagon.

The wagon train then crossed into the desert region, which was flat and arid. People talked about what they had longed for on the trip and what they were going to do when they got to California. The mood of the people on the wagon train was great, and spirits were elevated.

One night the wagon scout came galloping into camp, jumped off his horse, and pulled the wagon master aside. He told the wagon master that a few miles up ahead, a group of bandits had made camp right off the trail the wagons were traveling. He said, "There's mean and ornery thieves lurking out there! I'm a-feared they'll take everything we got!"

The wagon master thought and thought and, shaking his head, said he would sleep on it and figure it out in the morning.

Emmett listened to the conversation about the bandits. Emmett knew what he had to do, and he set about doing it. While everyone was asleep, he tiptoed out of camp and trotted off down the trail. Sure enough, there was a campfire, and some men were sitting around it, talking about the wagon train. The men spotted Emmett, but did that stop him? No how, no way! Emmett jumped and jumped and jumped up and down until the earth underneath him shivered and cracked and split apart, leaving the thieves on one side of the giant crevice and him and the trail on the other.

The next morning the wagon train passed the giant crevice in the ground. There was no evidence that anyone had been there. The wagon master was certain now that the scout had nothing but rocks in his head.

It was hot in the desert—unbearably hot—hotter than anyone had expected. The sun was burning down on the pioneers, making their faces look like red beets. The oxen were tired, and no one had the strength, much less desire, to talk. Children whined and complained and their mothers couldn't quiet them. There was not much farther to go on this long, long trek, but it sure felt to folks like it would take forever.

The wagon master decided to stop the day's travel and let everyone get a good night's rest. He and the wagon scout talked about the heat and the dust. The scout said, "It's so hot out here! I'm a-feared we'll bake like pies in an oven!"

The wagon master thought and thought and, shaking his head, said he would sleep on it and figure it out in the morning.

Emmett was too hot to sleep, and he overheard the wagon master and the scout talking. He knew what he had to do, and he set about doing it. While everyone was asleep, he tiptoed out of camp and trotted on down the trail, keeping his eyes peeled for a way to relieve the miserable heat.

He spotted some prickly-pear cactus and got a brilliant idea. There were thorns all over them, but did that stop Emmett? No how, no way! He gathered hundreds of cactus plants in his hands and stuck them all together to make one giant fan. As he moved the fan up and down, it generated a breeze. The gentle breeze wafted through the desert all the way to the wagon train, cooling everything and everyone.

Since everyone on the wagon train had cooled off and gotten a good night's sleep, they were ready to tackle the rest of the desert and the last leg of the journey. It helped that they had only about fifty miles to go.

The wagon scout reported back every night that it was smooth sailing from there on out. (Admittedly this made the wagon master nervous, since the scout had been wrong every other time.)

Then something happened that the scout could not have foreseen. When the train was about twenty miles from their destination, a rickety wheel on the wagon master's wagon broke, splintering into a million pieces. The wagon train came to a halt. No one could believe it. After all this time and with only a little bit left to go, they were held up by a broken wheel.

Everyone argued about what to do. One group thought they should stay and try to repair the wheel. The other thought they should divide the wagon master's things among them and abandon his wagon. What would they do with the oxen, though? Who would take what?

Emmett knew what he had to do, and he set about doing it. He trotted over to the broken-down wagon and curled himself around the axle. He knew they had twenty miles to go, but did that stop him? No how, no way! With a yell to the oxen to giddyup, the wagon lurched forward on three wheels and Emmett. The wagon train was back in business, and before you knew it, the train had crossed over the border and into California. They had done it—they had made the trip from St. Louis to California and lived to tell the tale!

So what ever happened to those pioneers? Well, they finally realized that it had been Emmett who had helped them out all along on the long journey. It was that last bit when he had made himself into a wheel that had done it.

"Why did you help us, Emmett?" they asked while thanking him.

Emmett told them that his African name was Emeka, which meant "Great Deeds." He said, "I have been able to do great deeds for as long as I can remember, and my papa always told me to use my strengths to help people. So I did and I do." Emmett grinned.

Later, when the people from the wagon train settled in California, they built a statue of Emmett for their town with a plaque that read, "Thanks to Emeka."

And what about Emmett? Well, he thought one wagon train trip was enough for anyone's lifetime. He opened up a general store, much like the one he had had in St. Louis. The wagon master retired and helped Emmett in the store part-time. He was not about to go on another wagon train trip without Emmett, even if the wagon master finally knew his scout wasn't crazy.

The wagon scout opened a sightseeing business in another city. He came back to the pioneers' town once a year to see his old friends. They traded stories about their adventures on the wagon train. Each time someone told a story, Emmett's great deeds grew even greater, but no one ever told anyone outside their group about the trip. You kinda had to be on that trip to believe it, so there wasn't much point in telling anyone else.

Until now.

Vocabulary

prairie (prâ´ rē) (page 6) *n.* A large area of level or rolling land with grass and few or no trees.

procession (prə sesh´ ən) (page 9) *n.* A group of persons moving forward in a line or in a certain order.

rationed (rash´ ənd) (page 14) *v.* Past tense of **ration:** To limit to fixed portions.

ladles (lā´ dəlz) (page 15) *n.* Plural of **ladle:** A spoon with a long handle and a bowl shaped like a cup. It is used to scoop up liquids.

region (rē´ jən) (page 16) *n.* Any large area or territory.

longed (longd) (page 16) *v.* Past tense of **long:** To want very much; yearn.

lurking (lûr´ king) (page 16) *v.* A form of the verb **lurk:** To lie hidden and quiet, preparing to attack.

evidence (e´ və dəns) (page 17) *n.* Proof of something.

rickety (ri´ ki tē) (page 21) *adj.* Likely to fall or break; shaky.

Comprehension Focus: Predicting

1. Reread page twelve. What did you predict Emmett might do next?

2. What do you predict Emmett might do in the future? Why do you think so?